Type design by Jessica Dacher.
Typeset in Jennerik and ITC Bailey Sans.
Manufactured in France.
ISBN 0-8118-3088-8

Library of Congress Cataloging-in-Publication Data
Got, Yves.
Sam's big book of words / illustrated by Yves Got.
p. cm.
ISBN 0-8118-3088-8
1. Vocabulary—Juvenile literature. [1. Vocabulary.] I. Title.
PE1449 .G645 2001
428.1
00-011439

Distributed in Canada by Raincoast Books
9050 Shaughnessy Street, Vancouver, British Columbia V6P 6E5

10 9 8 7 6 5 4 3 2

Chronicle Books LLC
85 Second Street, San Francisco, California 94105

www.chroniclekids.com

Sam's BIG Book of Words

by Yves Got

Sam's suitcase

boots

swimsuit

overalls

T-shirt

pajamas

raincoat

jacket

cap

books

Sam helps his mom

toothbrush

glass

pirate hat

modeling
clay

fire
truck

ball

Traveling

in a car

in a hot-air
balloon

on a boat

on Dad's bike

in an airplane

on a train

At the Beach

a small ball

paddle

beach umbrella

hat

starfish

water bottle

beach blanket

sunglasses

surf-board

garbage can

food vendor

sand

green bucket

shovel

sand castle

Sam goes swimming

with Dad

with Mom

mask

fins

seagull

a big ball

inflatable raft

trampoline

binoculars

Sam's Family

Dad

Mom

cousins Max and Alex

Grandpa
and
Grandma

little sister
Sophie

baby

baby-sitter

friend Tom

On a Picnic

birds

wasp

tree

butterfly

mushrooms

squirrel

thermos

slices of bread

cherries

bread

picnic basket

cow

kite

sheep

frogs

ar of jam

flowers

pple

ant

On a Farm

cows

tractor

duck pond

rooster

haystack

egg

hens and chicks

lamb

pony

scarecrow

At the Store

oranges

mandarins

watermelon

apples

banana

balls

shovels

buckets

lettuce

shopping
cart

yogurt

milk

books

peppers   tomatoes

Weather

storm

rain

wind

sun

splashing in
a small pool

playing in
the grass

battling with swords

swinging on
the swing set

Sam's Treasures

blueberry
jam

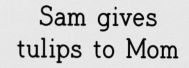
spinning
top

dried leaf

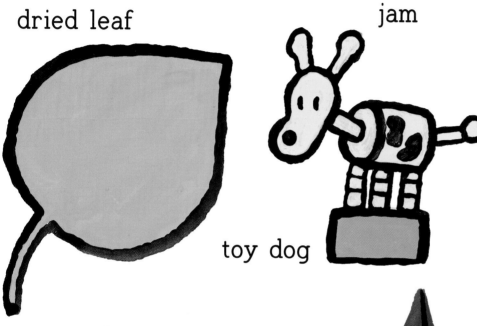

Sam gives
tulips to Mom

toy dog

teddy bear

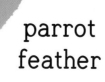
parrot
feather

snail

 a plastic
pirate

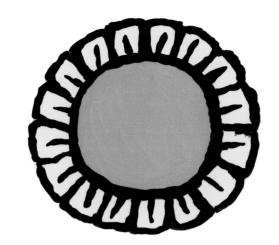 sunflower

 photo

 ladybug

seashells